Read to Me Again

Compiled by the

Child Study Association of America

READ-TO-ME STORYBOOK

READ ME ANOTHER STORY

READ ME MORE STORIES

HOLIDAY STORYBOOK

READ TO YOURSELF STORYBOOK

MORE READ TO YOURSELF STORIES:
    FUN AND MAGIC

CASTLES AND DRAGONS

READ TO ME AGAIN

NOW YOU CAN READ TO YOURSELF

Compiled by the

CHILD STUDY ASSOCIATION OF AMERICA

Read to
Me Again

Illustrated by Garry MacKenzie

THOMAS Y. CROWELL COMPANY · NEW YORK

6   7   8   9   10

ACKNOWLEDGMENTS

FOR PERMISSION TO REPRINT THE FOLLOWING COPYRIGHTED MATERIAL, GRATEFUL ACKNOWLEDGMENT AND THANKS ARE EXTENDED TO THE SOURCES INDICATED:

Abelard-Schuman Limited for "To Be a Duck" from *Up the Windy Hill* by Aileen Fisher, copyright 1953, and "When Company Comes" from *Runny Days, Sunny Days* by Aileen Fisher, copyright 1958.

Artists and Writers Press, Inc., for "Corally Crother's Birthday" by Romney Gay, published by Grosset & Dunlap, Inc., copyright 1944 by Phyllis Britcher.

Thomas Y. Crowell Company for "The Santa Claus Bears" by Dorothy Sherrill, copyright 1952 by Dorothy Sherrill, and "Where Have You Been?" by Margaret Wise Brown, copyright 1952 by Margaret Wise Brown.

Doubleday & Company, Inc., for "Tito's Hats" by Melchior G. Ferrer, copyright 1940 by Doubleday & Company, Inc., "Peter's Long Walk" by Lee Kingman, copyright 1953 by Mary Lee Natti, and "Me and the Bears" by Robert Bright, copyright 1951 by Robert Bright.

Doubleday & Company, Inc., and Harold Ober Associates Incorporated for "Angus and the Cat" by Marjorie Flack, copyright 1931 by Majorie Flack Larsson.

Doubleday & Company, Inc., and The World's Work Ltd. for "The Very Little Girl" by Phyllis Krasilovsky, copyright 1953 by Phyllis Krasilovsky.

E. P. Dutton & Co., Inc., for "Television" by Shirley Coran, from *Believe and Make Believe* by Lucy Sprague Mitchell and Irma Simonton Black, copyright © 1956 by the Bank Street College of Education; "Spring Rain," copyright 1946 by Marchette Chute, from the book *Around and About* by Marchette Chute, published 1957 by E. P. Dutton & Co., Inc.; "Doughnuts for Lin" by Nora S. Unwin, copyright 1950 by E. P. Dutton & Co., Inc.

Jeanne Hale for "Willie's Walk to Grandmama" by Margaret Wise Brown and Rockbridge Campbell.

Harcourt, Brace & World, Inc., for "Timothy Turtle," abridged from the book *Timothy Turtle* by Alice Vaught Davis, copyright 1940 by Harcourt, Brace & World, Inc.; "Reflection" from *Wide Awake and Other Poems*, © 1959 by Myra Cohn Livingston; "Morning" from *Whispers and Other Poems*, © 1958 by Myra Cohn Livingston.

Harper & Brothers for *But Not Billy* by Charlotte Zolotow, copyright 1947 by Harper & Brothers.

Barbara Bates Howell for "Good Morning" by Fannie R. Buchanan.

Margaret O. Hyde for "Little Lost Duck."

J. B. Lippincott Company for "The Baby House" by Norma Simon, copyright 1955 by Norma Simon, and "The Red Skirt" from *Mrs. Goose of Animal Town*, copyright 1939 by Miriam Clark Potter.

For our children
    and their children

PREFACE

In *Read to Me Again* the Children's Book Committee of the Child Study Association of America has once again brought together a collection chosen especially for young listeners. Here are thirty-six read-aloud stories and poems for many moods and occasions: bedtime stories and stories for a quiet afternoon, funny stories, magic stories and stories about the here and now—all gaily illustrated by Garry MacKenzie.

Read-aloud time is a special time for many of us—for reader and listener alike. For parents it may be a time of special closeness, of genuine sharing in their children's first glimpses of the joy and wonder in books. For an older brother or sister, reading aloud to the youngest may mean a new pride in accomplishment, a sudden awareness that a newly won skill can give pleasure to others. And, for young listeners themselves, the stories first heard and loved at home bring a particular delight.

Read to Me Again was compiled for just such pleasures.

A. D. BUCHMUELLER
Executive Director
Child Study Association of America

Contents

Read to Me Again

Morning

MYRA COHN LIVINGSTON

Everyone is tight asleep,
I think I'll sing a tune,
And if I sing it loud enough
I'll wake up someone—soon!

When You Were a Little Baby

RHODA A. BERMAN

When you were a little baby,
A tiny little baby,
A just born baby,
A brand new baby,
Just the kind of baby
We always wished we had . . .

You didn't have any hair.
You didn't have any teeth.
You were very small and fat.
You had wrinkles and crinkles.
Now, what do you think of that?
Oh, you don't believe it?
Ask your Mommy—she ought to know!

You couldn't sit.
You couldn't talk.
You couldn't laugh.
You couldn't walk.
Oh, you don't believe it?
Ask your Daddy—he ought to know!

Mommy fed you upon her lap.
And while you ate you took a nap.
And when we put you in your bath
You'd laugh and laugh and laugh and laugh!

You threw your dishes on the floor.
We're glad you don't do *that* any more!
You had a chest full of toys
And lots of other things
For baby girls and boys.

Your favorite game was peek-a-boo
When everybody looked for you.
And once you reached up for the moon
As though it were a big balloon
Just meant for you!

You got bigger every day.
You could talk.
You could walk.
You could climb upon a chair.
You could even comb your hair.
You grew and grew and grew and grew.
And now see all the things you do!
But you'll get bigger and bigger still
Just as all new babies will.
YOU WAIT AND SEE!

"Scat, Scat"

SALLY R. FRANCIS

Once there was a little pussy cat
who hadn't any home . . .
She had a pink little nose
and soft little toes.

One day she went walking down the street
crying "Me-ow, me-ow,"
and by and by she came to an old woman
sweeping the sidewalk.

"Me-ow, me-ow," said the little cat,
but when the old woman saw her
she took her broom
and swept the little cat out into the street.

"Scat, scat, go 'way, little cat,"
said the old woman,
and the little cat rolled over in the dust.

She was dirt
from her pink little nose to her soft little toes,
but she got up and walked away.

After a while she saw a man with a hose.
He was sprinkling the flowers in his garden.

And when the little cat saw him she said,
"Me-ow, me-ow."
But when the man saw the cat
he was very angry.
He turned the hose on her and said,
"Scat, scat,
Go 'way, little cat!"

The poor little cat was wet
from her pink little nose
to her soft little toes,
but she got up and walked away.

The little cat didn't know where to go,
so she sat down
and looked all around.

Very soon along came a black dog.
"Bow-wow-wow," said the black dog and
"Scat, scat, I'll catch you, cat!"

The little cat ran and the big dog ran after her.
They ran and ran until they came to a fence.

Then up jumped the little white cat,
and the black dog said, "Bow-wow-wow."
But he couldn't jump up on the fence
and he soon grew tired of barking.
So he lay down to rest and took a nap.

After a while the little cat crept very very softly
along the fence
and then jumped down and ran away.

By and by she came to a door and it was open,
so in walked the little cat.
On a table she saw a big white cake
with frosting on it.
But when the lady saw a cat in her kitchen
she was very angry.
She got a stick and chased her out, saying,
"Scat, scat,
Go 'way, little cat!"

And away she ran.
When she had gone a long way she saw a window,
and on the window sill was a flower box
filled with flowers. Into it jumped the little cat
and sat down among the flowers.

The flower box belonged to Rosy Runabout
and when she saw the little cat in it
she called to her mother and said,
"Oh Mother, come and see this sweet little cat!"
Rosy Runabout took the little white cat in her arms
and hugged her tight and said,
"I am going to have you for my very own little cat!"
And the little white cat said, "Purr-purr-purr."

So the little white cat with the pink little nose
and the soft little toes
went to live with Rosy Runabout
and every morning
she drank her milk from a little blue bowl.

And when she was a very good little cat
Rosy Runabout took her riding in her doll carriage.

And no one ever said,
"Scat, scat,
Go 'way, little cat!" again.

Me and the Bears

ROBERT BRIGHT

It's fun at the zoo.

I like the big elephant
and the tall giraffe
and the funny kangaroo.

But best of all I like the little BEARS

Because I think
they could come to my house
and play with me.

What fun that would be!
The little bears at my house.

But in my house
when I'm undressed
I look upstairs
everywheres
for BEARS
But there are NO bears—
just chairs and things.

My mother comes upstairs
and reads a story.
But there is nothing about
BEARS.
Just woolly sheep to make me sleep.

And so I say my prayers
for Papa, Mama, and for me,
but especially for the
BEARS.

And then I try to go to sleep
this way,
thinking about bears,

and that way,
wishing I had bears,

and even
this
way,
till I guess
I'm awfully sleepy
thinking about bears.

But then I think I hear a noise
in my house
and I think it is the mouse
that lives in our house,

But it's the BEARS.

They have come to visit me
and to dance with me,
to dress up in my clothes,
to play blindman's buff,
and to make a lot of noise.

Oh, me and the bears
we have all kinds of fun
UNTIL
the mouse wakes up.

And we have to hide,
me and the bears.
So then we are very quiet.

And we read a story,
me and the bears.
And the story is all about
BEARS
and
ME

And then we say
our prayers
me and the bears.

And when the moon comes up
we're fast asleep
ME
and
the little BEARS.

Holding Hands

LENORE M. LINK

Elephants walking
Along the trails

Are holding hands
By holding tails.

Trunks and tails
Are handy things

When elephants walk
In circus rings.

Elephants work
And elephants play

And elephants walk
And feel so gay.

And when they walk—
It never fails—

They're holding hands
By holding tails.

14

The Very Little Girl

PHYLLIS KRASILOVSKY

Once there was a little girl
who was very very very little.

She was smaller than a rose bush.
She was smaller than a kitchen stool.
She was smaller than her mother's work basket.

She couldn't see over the garden fence.
She couldn't see the face on the grandfather clock.
She couldn't even reach a door handle!

She had to have
a special little chair to sit on

15

and a special little table to eat on
and a special little bed to sleep on.

She was smaller
than all the other little girls she played with.
She was smaller than anyone on her street!

BUT ONE DAY
SHE COULD REACH THE FISH BOWL!

She could lift up her cat.
She was bigger than her dog.
And bigger than a footstool!

Every day after that she found more things which
   were smaller than she.

The very little girl began to grow
B I G G E R !

She grew BIGGER than the rose bush.
And BIGGER than the kitchen stool.
And BIGGER than her mother's work basket.

She could see over the garden fence.
She could see the face on the grandfather clock.
She could even reach a door handle and open a door!

She grew too BIG
for her special little chair
and her special little table
and her special little bed.

Now she ate at the big table with her mother and
      daddy
And she had a new big bed!

She was no longer a very little girl.
She was the same size as
the other little girls she played with.
She didn't have to stand on tiptoe any more.

Now she was big enough
to be a big sister
to her brand new baby brother
who was very very very little!

Smart Little Kitty

LOUISE WOODCOCK

Peter was a little boy and he had a smart little kitty. The kitty could do lots of things . . .

She could chase her own funny little pointed tail—round and round and round.

Peter couldn't do that. Oh, no.

The kitty could make her hair stand right out straight when she was frightened.

Peter couldn't do that. Oh, no.

The kitty could jump from the floor high up onto the toy cupboard.

Peter couldn't do that. Oh, no.

The kitty could roll up into a tight little round ball when she went to sleep.

Peter couldn't do that. Oh, no.

He wished he could!

BUT . . .

Peter was a smart little boy.
He could do lots of things, too.
Peter could eat his cereal out of a spoon.

The kitty couldn't do that. Oh, no.

Peter could put on his overalls all alone, and even buckle up the straps.

The kitty couldn't do that. Oh, no.

Peter could build a tunnel with his blocks, and make his train go through it—chug-chug-chug.

The kitty couldn't do that. Oh, no.

Peter could read a book just like this one.

The kitty couldn't do that. Oh, no.

But that little kitty
DIDN'T EVEN CARE!

Television

SHIRLEY CORAN

When a funny man
Makes a funny face
On a television show,
I can make
A face right back—
AND HE WILL NEVER KNOW!

Reflection

MYRA COHN LIVINGSTON

In the mirror
I can see
Lots of things
But mostly—me.

Hello, Helicopter

ETHEL KESSLER

Round go the wheels
  of the automobiles.
  Round   round   round.

And the great big trucks
  with their thick double wheels
  go round   round   round.
  Down the street and over the highways
  they zoom with a roaring sound.

Round goes a whirling wheel in the sky.
  Round   round   round.

First I hear it; then I see it
Twirling, whirling, around spins the
  great propeller on top of the helicopter.

Bruum-ummmmmmmmm goes the rotor.
Bruummmmmmmmm.
It's flying lower and lower
  Can the pilot see me?

I can see the rotor turning like a
  giant windmill in the sky.
Like a merry-go-round.
  Round   round.

But the helicopter can go
   straight up
   and straight down, too
   Up. Down.
   Going up. Going down.
   Like an elevator.
It can go from side to side too.
It can stop in mid-air and just stay there

Did you ever see an airplane just
  stop in the sky?
STOP! Stop for me!
  Fly low. So low that I can see you.
  Where are you going?
  What are you bringing today?
Are you loaded with fresh fish just caught
  from the sea?
Are you carrying bananas and cherries and
  ripe, red strawberries?
Are you bringing a new kangaroo to the zoo?
No!
You are loaded with sacks.
You are full of heavy packs.
Well, what is the helicopter bringing?
Oh, now I can tell.
I see on the side, printed in blue,
  "U.S. Mail."
Will there be a letter for me?
And maybe one for you?

The Red Skirt

MIRIAM CLARK POTTER

It was a cold winter day. Mrs. Goose said to herself, "I think I will make myself a nice new red skirt. That will keep me warm and cozy."

She looked out of the window; the snow was blowing in little fluffs and flurries right against the icy glass. "Oh, how cold it is!" Mrs. Goose shivered. "Quite too chilly to go over to Mr. Gobbler's store to buy some red cloth for my skirt."

Then she wondered: "Have I something woolly and bright and thick, right here in the house, that I could make my skirt out of?"

She rushed to her shelf to look. Yes, there was an old red blanket, very rough and heavy.

"This will do nicely," thought Mrs. Goose, and she got out her scissors and needle and thread and set to work at once. "I'll cut it in two, like this—" She snipped. "Then one half will do to wrap around me and sew up, and the other half will be left over."

So there sat Mrs. Goose, basting and stitching, and before she knew it, the skirt was done. She even sewed buttons on it. She put it right on; and although it dragged way down behind, she felt that she looked very fine in it.

"It's stopped snowing now," she said, peering through the window. "I'll run right along and show my fine new skirt to my friends. What hat shall I wear, I wonder."

After a while she chose a queer tight one, opened the front door, and locked it behind her.

But oh, dear; what was the matter? Mrs. Goose could not budge an inch; every time she tried to go away from the door, something pulled her back.

"Very strange, very strange," she thought. "What is the matter? I must have locked the door on my long skirt. What shall I do? I can't stay *here* all night."

She thought and thought, and finally she said to herself: "I know. I'll unfasten my skirt and take it off. Then I can go on, free."

So she wriggled out and went off, without looking back. Mrs. Goose plopped along in her white petticoat, feeling very cold.

"Where was I going, anyway?" she asked herself. "Oh, I was going to show my friends my new skirt. But I had to take it off! So what's the use of going, anyway? I think I'll plop home."

So Mrs. Goose started back; but as she got near her house she saw a red thing hanging from her door, blowing back and forth in the wind.

"Fire," said Mrs. Goose, feeling frightened. "No, a red flag. That means danger. What is the matter in my house? Had I better run for help?"

She stretched her long neck and blinked her black eyes, and then she recognized her own new skirt, woolly and bright and thick. "How silly of me!" said Mrs. Goose, and went up to her door, laughing. "How could I forget?"

She took the key out of her pocket and unlocked the door. Of course the skirt fell out then. "I was very foolish," said Mrs. Goose. "I might have done this before. Well, this time I'll put my skirt on and go along; it is not too late to show it to my friends."

Mrs. Squirrel's house had blue smoke coming out of the chimney. When the door was opened, there was a good smell of things baking. Mrs. Squirrel was a little tired and flurried. "Come in, Mrs. Goose," she said, "and have a bit of fresh bread with butter on it. But what on earth have you got on? It looks like a blanket."

That made Mrs. Goose a little cross. "It *was* a blanket," she said, "but now it is a skirt. How do you like it?" She turned round and round before Mrs. Squirrel. "I made it this very afternoon. Just what I wanted; something woolly and bright and thick."

"Well, it certainly is woolly," said Mrs. Squirrel. "And bright and thick too. I still think it looks a little like a blanket. But if you are pleased, that is all right, Mrs. Goose."

"Good-by then," said Mrs. Goose, walking off. Her skirt dragged across the floor. "Thank you for the bite to eat."

She plopped along the snowy street. White flakes had begun to fall again. There was Black Cat from Green Street, going to the store for some groceries, with his snowshoes on.

"Why, hello there, Mrs. Goose," he said. "When I first saw you coming, I thought you were a fire engine. How very big you look, and red against the snow. What is that, a new dress? Why is it so long?"

"It's a new skirt," said Mrs. Goose, not quite liking what Black Cat had said. "Woolly and bright and thick. Don't you like it?"

"Well, it certainly is bright," said Black Cat with a queer smile, skidding around the corner with his basket, "and it certainly is long, and it does look *thick*."

"What does he mean, saying 'bright' and 'long' and 'thick' like that?" wondered Mrs. Goose. "Well, I'll go on to Three-Ducks' house. They will be glad to see me this cold winter day."

So she went tapping at their door.

There was no answer; they were not at home.

Mrs. Goose was so disappointed that she hunched down on their cold doorstep and shut her black eyes.

"What an awful time I am having with my new skirt," she said. "First it got locked in—then Mrs. Squirrel said it looked like a blanket—then Black Cat said it was so bright. And now Three-Ducks are not at home. Well, I'll just sit here until they come."

It began to snow harder. Mrs. Goose got up and shook big flakes off her new red skirt. Just as she was doing that she heard a quacking; there were Three-Ducks. They were coming back from Blue Pond and they looked very cold.

"Hello, Mrs. Goose," they said. "Did you come to see us?"

"Yes," said Mrs. Goose. "But it is getting dark; and how cold it is!"

"Come in, and we will build a fire," said Three-Ducks. So they all went into the house. It was dark there, and chilly. But when the fire flared up, it shone over the red thing that Mrs. Goose was wearing. "Why, you have a new skirt!" quacked Three-Ducks, all together.

"I made it this very afternoon," said Mrs. Goose. "These winter days I need something woolly and bright and thick. Why, the winds just whistle across Blue Pond, and the Hopping-Green is all frozen up!"

Three-Ducks pecked at the skirt a bit. "It is thick,"

they said. "Doesn't it drag too much, Mrs. Goose? Isn't it a little heavy, for a skirt?"

"Certainly it doesn't drag too much," Mrs. Goose told them, trailing it across the floor. "And I like it heavy."

"Oh," said Three-Ducks. "Well, have it as you wish. Now let's have some tea."

They had their tea there by the fire, and Mrs. Goose got very hot with her big red skirt on. When she got up she tripped over it, and her cup went flying to the floor.

"I'm glad it didn't break," she said. "Well, I must go now. Thank you for the tea."

When she got to her house it was very cold there. The fire had gone out. "Oh, dear!" Mrs. Goose said to herself, "I shall need an extra cover tonight. I wish I had not cut the red blanket up and made a skirt of it. Here is the other half—right on the table. Well, it is very simple, really. I'll just rip up the skirt, take the buttons off, sew the pieces together, and make a blanket of it again!"

So she did that, sewing till she was very sleepy and chilled. Then she put on her long gray nightgown and went to bed, with the red blanket on top.

"This is better," said Mrs. Goose, yawning. "Woolly and bright and thick; woolly and bright and thick. Mrs. Squirrel was right; the Black Cat from Green Street was right; Three-Ducks were right. It is better as a blanket, really."

And she shut her eyes and went to sleep, that cold winter night.

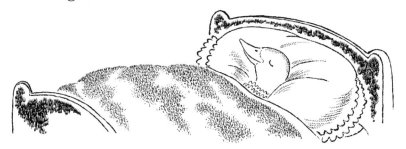

Where Have You Been?

MARGARET WISE BROWN

Little Old Cat
Little Old Cat
Where have you been?
To see this and that
Said the Little Old Cat
That's where I've been.

Little Old Squirrel
Little Old Squirrel
Where have you been?
I've been out on a whirl
Said the Little Old Squirrel
That's where I've been.

Little Old Fish
Little Old Fish
Where do you swim?
Where I wish
Said the Little Old Fish
That's where I swim.

Little Brown Bird
Little Brown Bird
Where do you fly?
I fly in the sky
Said the Little Brown Bird
That's where I fly.

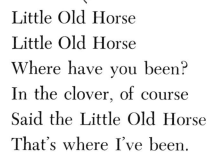

Little Old Horse
Little Old Horse
Where have you been?
In the clover, of course
Said the Little Old Horse
That's where I've been.

Little Old Toad
Little Old Toad
Where have you been?
I've been way up the road
Said the Little Old Toad
That's where I've been.

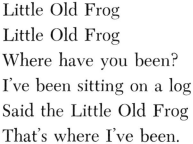

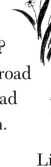

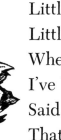

Little Old Frog
Little Old Frog
Where have you been?
I've been sitting on a log
Said the Little Old Frog
That's where I've been.

Little Old Mole
Little Old Mole
Where have you been?
Down a long dark hole
Said the Little Old Mole
That's where I've been.

Little Old Bunny
Little Old Bunny
Why do you run?
I run because it's fun
Said the Little Old Bunny
That's why I run.

Little Old Mouse
Little Old Mouse
Why run down the clock?
To see if the tick
Comes after the tock
I run down the clock.

Shiny Red Boots

CATHERINE WOOLLEY

Every morning when Bobby got up his mother said, "Get dressed, dear. Put on your shoes. Tie your shoelaces."

Every morning Bobby said, "Where are my shoes?"

Every morning Mother said, "Where did you leave them?"

Bobby said, "I don't remember."

Mother said, "You never remember."

"Oh, here's one shoe down in this chair!" Bobby said.

"Did you drop the other in the hall?" asked Mother.

"When will you ever," she said with a great big sigh, "put your shoes in the closet or neatly under the bed!"

On Bobby's birthday he got a pair of boots—shiny red rubber boots.

Mother said, "We'll put these boots in your closet until you need them."

Next morning when Bobby got up his mother said, "Get dressed, dear. Put on your shoes."

Bobby found one shoe half way downstairs, the other under his pillow. He was just going to put them on when he remembered his boots, his shiny red rubber boots.

So he put his shoes under the bed, neatly side by side.

He put his boots on.

He went clump, clumping to breakfast.

Daddy said, "Good morning, Butch. And why have you got your boots on this fine day?"

Bobby looked down at his shiny red boots. They twinkled at him. He couldn't quite think why he had them on but he knew there was some good reason.

He said, "Because."

He wiggled his boots to make them twinkle while he ate.

After breakfast Bobby went clump, clumping out to play.

He saw Emily. She said, "Bobby, it isn't cold. Why have you got your boots on?"

Bobby watched his boots twinkle. He said, "Because."

He rode his bike. He met Mrs. Stuart. She said, "Bobby, it isn't raining. Why have you got your boots on?"

Bobby said, "Because."

He met the mailman. The mailman said, "Bobby, it isn't muddy today. Why have you got your boots on?"

Bobby said, "Because."

He rode his bike home, watching his boots twinkle.

Mother said, "Come on, we're going to the store."

The man in the store saw Bobby. He saw the red rubber boots.

He said, "Hello, Boots! Where are you going with that cowboy?"

Bobby looked at the man and looked at his boots and looked at the man again. Now he knew the reason!

He said to Mother on the way home, "Know why I'm wearing my new red boots?"

"No. Why?" said Mother.

"Because I'm a cowboy," Bobby said.

When he got home he went clump, clumping to Emily's house.

He said, "Know why I'm wearing my new red boots?"

"No. Why?" said Emily.

"Because I'm a cowboy," Bobby said.

He went clump, clumping to Mrs. Stuart's.

He said, "Know why I'm wearing my new red boots?"

"Why are you?" said Mrs. Stuart.

"Because I'm a cowboy, of course," Bobby said.

He went clump, clumping home.

Mother said, "Come on, we're going to have our nap."

They went into Bobby's bedroom.

Bobby said, "Do cowboys take naps?"

Mother said, "They certainly do!"

Bobby got undressed, all but his boots. He said, "Do cowboys wear their boots to bed when they take their naps?"

Mother said, "They certainly don't! They put their boots under the bed, neatly, side by side, so they can find them quick when the head cowboy calls them."

Bobby said, "Oh."

He took off his boots.

He saw his shoes under the bed where he had put them that morning. He said, "I'll put my shoes in the closet in case I need them again."

He put his boots under the bed very, very neatly.

"That's the way cowboys always do," said Bobby as he bounced into bed.

Spring Rain

MARCHETTE CHUTE

The storm came up so very quick
   It couldn't have been quicker.
I should have brought my hat along,
   I should have brought my slicker.

My hair is wet, my feet are wet,
   I couldn't be much wetter.
I fell into a river once
   But this is even better.

Little Lost Duck

MARGARET O. HYDE

Once there was a duck egg that rolled into the pig pen.

Peck, peck. Crackety, crack. The egg opened and a little duck came out. He was all alone among the pigs. There was not another duck in sight.

Oink oink said the pigs as they sniffed in the trough for their dinner.

The little duck listened and tried to say oink. But no matter how hard he tried, the only noise he could make was QUACK.

"This is not the place for me," said the little duck. "This is not my family."

42

So the lonesome little duck walked through a hole in the fence of the pig pen. He waddled along until he came to the cows who were nibbling on the green grass in the meadow. The grass was so green and tender that they didn't notice the little duck.

Then one of the cows lifted her head and said moo in a great loud voice. A little calf said moo moo in a much higher voice.

When the little duck tried to moo he quacked.

"I do not belong with these animals," said the duck.

He waddled over to the place where the sheep were napping. One of them stood up slowly and said baa very softly. Then some other sheep awoke and walked around the meadow. The little duck watched them and listened.

Baa baa said the sheep. Baa baa.

The little duck tried to baa like the sheep. But what kind of a noise do you think he made?

"My quack does not sound like a baa," said the duck. "This is not the home for me."

Not far away, a horse was resting his head on a fence. The duck watched him for a long time. The horse was very quiet. He did not make any noise at all. Then a big truck rumbled down the road. The horse lifted his head. Neigh neigh he said.

Quack quack answered the duck as he walked toward the chicken yard to look for his home.

The baby chicks were snuggled close to their mother. Cheep cheep, cheep cheep, they said.

Some of the chickens were pecking at the corn. Cluck cluck went one of the chickens. Cluck cluck.

Cackle cackle said a big, old hen.

Cock a doodle doo crowed the rooster.

"This place would make a fine home," said the duck.

So the duck tried to cheep and he tried to cluck. He tried to cackle and to cock a doodle doo. But no matter how hard he tried, every time he opened his mouth, out came a quack.

While the duck was wondering where to go next big drops of rain began to fall.

The rain splashed the chickens in the chicken yard. The chickens went into their house.

The rain made puddles in the pig pen.

The pigs squealed and splashed in the mud.

The cows gathered under the big tree in the meadow and used it for an umbrella.

The horse went back to his stall to keep dry. This was not good weather for horses.

But it was fine weather for ducks.

The little lost duck swam happily through the big puddles. Quack quack he sang as he came to the pond. He dove right in. What fun he had swimming in the rain!

And there on the pond was a whole family of ducks. Five little ducks were swimming happily behind their mother. The little lost duck joined the line and swam along with them.

Then something wonderful happened. All at once the ducks said quack.

The little lost duck said quack loudest of all, for he knew that he had found his family. He would never be lonesome any more.

But Not Billy

CHARLOTTE ZOLOTOW

Once there was a mother who had a new baby. His name was Billy but she never called him that.

When he was hungry he cried without tears for his dinner—aaaaaaack, aaaaaaaack, aaaaaaaaaaaaack—and he sounded the way little ducks sound when they quack across blue summer ponds. So she called him little duck,

but not Billy.

When he had almost finished his milk, his eyes half closed and he cooed, oooooooh, ooooohhhhhh, oooooo-

ooooooooooohhhhhhhhhhh,   with   sleepiness.   He
sounded like a pigeon in the sunlight. So she called
him little pigeon,

> but not Billy.

When he fell asleep on his stomach with his legs
bent out from each side he looked like a little frog.
So she called him little frog,

> but not Billy.

When he was wide awake and alone in his crib he
would lie on his back and hold his foot in his hand and
sing zzzzzzzzzzzzzzz zzzzzzzzzzzz to himself. That
is the sound honey bees sing in fields of clover. So
she called him little bee,

> but not Billy.

When he got up on his knees and leaned on his
hands and rocked back and forth in the play pen, he
looked like a busy little rocking horse. So she called
him little rocking horse,

> but not Billy.

When he began to sit, he held himself up by lean-
ing forward on his two arms, looking up with great
solemn eyes like an owl's. So she called him little owl,

> but not Billy.

When he tried to stand up he couldn't, so he wob-
bled forward on all fours like an awkward little bear
cub in the woods. So she called him little bear,
but not Billy.

When she gave him a carrot to chew he held it with
his hands and wrinkled up his nose like a bunny. So
she called him little bunny,
but not Billy.

When she put him into his warm bath at night, he
kicked and splashed and shot back and forth in the
water like a little fish in a forest stream. So she called
him little fish,
but not Billy.

Then one day he did something that no little animal and no little bird and no little insect and no little fish can do. It was something only a little baby can do.

His mother came to see why he was quiet so long. He was standing up in his play pen watching the door. When he caught sight of her he said, mmmmm-mmmmmmmmmmm MA MA

His mother picked him up and hugged him and called him

        not little bunny, not little bear
        not little duck, not little owl
        not little fish, not little frog
        not little pigeon, not little bee
        not little rocking horse
            but

BILLY!

The Ba-Ba Blanket

LOUISE FILER SCHLOSS

Nancy was a very little girl
Just two years old.
She was busy all day long.
There was so much to see.
Her eyes were filled with looking.
There was so much to hear.
Her ears were always listening.
There was so much to smell.
Her nose was busy sniffing.
But sometimes everything was too big for Nancy,
too strange and too noisy and too fast.

Grownups looked like giants with long legs, their
faces 'way, 'way up toward the sky.

Nancy's Mommy understood. She knew how it must seem to be a little girl in a big world.

Nancy's Mommy had a nice wide lap for sitting.

Nancy's Daddy understood too.

After breakfast, he would swing Nancy up high on his shoulders.

Sometimes he took her for a long ride on his shoulders. Then she could look down on all the big people. Nancy grabbed Daddy's hair and screamed with excitement.

"More, Daddy, more!"

"That's all for today," Daddy said. "I must go to my office."

He gave her a kiss and a hug and off he went.

Then Nancy looked for her Mommy.

Mommy was indoors making the beds.

"Hi, dear," Mommy said. And went right on making beds.

That was when Nancy looked for her blanket, the one that she called her Ba-Ba. The Ba-Ba was soft and nice to hold. Once it had been bright pink with blue teddy bears marching across it, but that was long ago.

By the time Nancy was two years old Ba-Ba was a mousy, muddy color, and the teddy bears had faded away.

But Nancy didn't care about that—she loved her blanket. It felt just right. Safe and warm and friendly. Never grumpy or just too busy. Always the same. The minute Nancy touched it she felt happy.

When she was a tiny baby, her very first word—the first word she had ever spoken—was "Ba-Ba."

"Ba-Ba, Ba-Ba," baby Nancy had said, over and over again, "Ba-Ba, Ba-Ba."

And then Mommy knew she wanted her blanket.

Days went by. Soon Nancy learned to walk and to talk. She toddled about, running from one thing to another, touching, tasting, smelling. Everywhere that Nancy went, her Ba-Ba blanket went too. It went with her to the sand pile, and got mixed up in the mud pies. The Ba-Ba hung over her high chair and caught bits of carrot and custard as they slipped off the spoon. Once the Ba-Ba blew out of the car window and was nearly lost but Daddy saw it just in time. He fished it out of a thick pool of oil. Now the Ba-Ba was more grubby and greasy and grimy than ever.

One day Grandma-from-far-away was coming to visit.

"My, what a fine big girl you're getting to be," said Grandma, and she gave Nancy a starchy kiss.

Then Mommy and Grandma talked so busily to each other that they didn't talk to Nancy at all. Nancy helped herself to a cookie. She took a big bite. She stared at Grandma and took another bite. She held on to the cookie in one hand, twisting and turning the Ba-Ba with the other. Suddenly Grandma said to Mommy:

"How can you allow that child to carry such a dirty blanket around?"

Early next morning Mommy put the blanket into the washing machine. When she hung it up to dry there was the good smell of soap and water. Nancy was very unhappy. Tears were in her eyes. She wanted her Ba-Ba.

Mommy did not know what to do.

"I want my Ba-Ba. I want my Ba-Ba," she whined until lunch. After lunch, Mommy pulled the blanket down from the line. It was still wet.

It was time for her nap and Mommy put Nancy in her crib.

Now she began to cry big tears.

"Ba-Ba. Give me Ba-Ba."

Now Mommy had a fine idea. She warmed the oven
and put the Ba-Ba blanket inside to dry. At this very
moment the telephone rang. It was Aunt Tillie.
Mommy talked and talked. Suddenly she remembered: "Goodness, gracious. The Ba-Ba blanket is in
the oven!" She hung up the telephone and didn't even
say good-by to Aunt Tillie.

Sure enough, one end of the blanket was burned.
The rest was still a little damp. Mommy took the scissors and snipped off the burned part. She put what
was left of it in the crib. Nancy put her cheek against
it and went right to sleep.

Many things happened after that. Once the blanket
got caught in the radiator. Nancy yanked and pulled.
The Ba-Ba came loose all right but a big piece was
torn off.

Another time there was a boy in the park with a
frisky puppy. The puppy wanted to play. When Nancy
ran with the Ba-Ba in her hand the puppy ran after
her. All at once he snatched the blanket with his teeth.
The blanket tore and the puppy scampered off with
a large piece of the Ba-Ba blanket hanging from his
mouth.

Still another time—in the summer—the Ba-Ba blanket was lying on a table on the porch. A bird hopped across the table. He looked at the blanket a moment. Then he gave it a quick nip and pulled off a piece. Away he flew with the piece of blanket in his beak to make a warm padding for his nest.

In time, the Ba-Ba blanket became a tiny piece of cloth even smaller than a handkerchief. As Nancy grew bigger, the blanket grew littler.

Soon it was Nancy's birthday. It was her doll's birthday too. Betsy Doll had come when Nancy was born, so they were both three years old on the same birthday.

Nancy felt bigger now that she was three.

She was big enough to sit at the dinner table with her Mommy and Daddy.

She could ride a tricycle alone.

She could dress herself almost all alone.

And best of all, she was big enough to go to nursery school!

The birthday party was over, the candles had been blown out, and the children had all gone home when Nancy remembered. She remembered the present for Betsy. She had thought and thought about it. It was in her bathrobe pocket—a tiny package wrapped in scribbled crayon paper and tied with a piece of Christmas ribbon.

She took it out now. "Would you like me to open it for you, Betsy?" she asked.

Nancy slipped the ribbon off carefully. The paper fell apart. Inside was all that remained of the Ba-Ba blanket. Nancy stuffed it into Betsy's toy pocketbook.

"I'm a big girl now. *You* can use it for a hankie," Nancy explained. "Happy birthday!"

To Be a Duck

AILEEN FISHER

It must be fun to be a duck
and row yourself around
and race with others nip and tuck
and make a quacky sound,
and dribble water through your beak,
and wear a jacket white and sleek,
and be too waterproof to leak.

It must be fun to float and float
around and in between,
and when you're tired of being a boat
to be a submarine
and chase the minnows and the fish,
or take off with a whirry swish
and be an airplane, if you wish.

Angus and the Cat

MARJORIE FLACK

Each day as Angus grew older, he grew longer but not much higher. Scottie dogs grow that way.

Now as Angus grew older and longer he learned MANY THINGS.

He learned it is best to stay in one's own yard.

He learned that frogs can jump but dogs must NOT jump after them.

Angus also learned NOT to lie on the sofa and NOT to take somebody else's food and things like that.

Now there was something outdoors Angus was very curious about but had never learned about, and that was CATS. His leash was always too short.

Then one day what should Angus find indoors lying on the sofa but a strange little CAT!

Angus came closer.

The cat sat up.

Angus came closer.

Up jumped the cat onto the arm of the sofa. Angus came closer and—siss-s-s-s-s-s!!! That little cat boxed Angus's ears! Woo-oo-oof—woo-oo-oof! said Angus.

Up jumped the cat onto the sofa back, up to the mantel, and Angus was not high enough to reach her.

But at lunch time down she came to try and take Angus's food—though not for long.

Up she jumped onto the table, and Angus was not high enough to reach her.

At nap time there she was sitting in Angus's own special square of sunshine—washing her face—though not for long.

Up she jumped onto the window sill, and Angus was not high enough to reach her!

For three whole days Angus was very busy chasing that cat, but she always went up out of reach. On the fourth day he chased her up the stairs, and into the bedroom. But she was completely gone!

Angus looked under the bed. No cat was there.

Angus looked out of the window into his yard, into

the next yard, and the next. No cat was in sight.

Angus went down the stairs. He looked on the sofa. No cat was there. He looked on the mantel. No cat was there. Angus looked on the table and on the window sills. No cat was indoors a-n-y-w-h-e-r-e.

So Angus was all alone. There was no cat to box his ears. There was no cat to take his food. There was no cat to sit in his sunshine. There was no cat to chase away. So Angus had nothing to do!

Angus missed the little cat.

But at lunch time he heard a noise. *Purrrrr*. There she was again.

And Angus knew and the cat knew that Angus was glad the cat came back!

Peter's Long Walk

LEE KINGMAN

Peter lived in the country.

Peter had a cat who danced about when he threw a ball to her.

Peter had a dog who splashed about when he threw sticks in the pond for him.

Peter had sheep who pattered up when he threw bread to them.

Peter had ducks who chattered up when he threw corn to them.

But Peter's house was away off by itself in the woods, and there wasn't another boy or girl who lived near enough to play with Peter.

Peter was as lonely as a chicken in an egg.

"You just wait," said Peter's mother. "When you are five years old and go to school in the village, you'll have someone to play with every day."

So Peter waited. He waited all the long, long year he was four. Finally, on a bright spring day, Peter grew up and was five!

But before he blew out the candles on his birthday cake, Peter thought a wish—the wish he always wished. "I wish I could find someone to play with me."

Peter looked at the five candles winking at him. Then he shut his eyes tight and blew, for if all the candles went out, his wish would come true.

But when he opened his eyes, he saw one candle still blinking at him! He must have blown right around a corner and missed it.

"Now my wish won't come true!" he cried.

Peter felt as lonely as an island in the sea.

"That just means it won't come true all by itself," Peter's mother said. "You'll have to make it come true all by *yourself* instead."

Then and there Peter made up his mind. His mother had said when he was five years old and went to school in the village he would have someone to play with him. So tomorrow he would go to the village and make his wish come true all by himself.

Early the next morning, before his mother was even awake, Peter ran out of the farmyard gate. He was off to the village to go to school.

For a while Peter trotted joyfully, but it was a long walk. After a while he sat down on a rock to rest.

Suddenly he knew someone was watching him. Perhaps it was someone who would play with him.

He turned around and looked around, but he couldn't see anything.

He felt a scared little shiver run down his back and up his back.

There was Peter, all by himself on a long walk, and he felt as lonely as a turtle in his shell.

But Peter was on his way to school at last. So he jumped up and trudged on hopefully. It was a long walk. After a while he sat down by a brook to rest.

Suddenly he knew someone was watching him. Perhaps it was someone who would play with him.

He turned around and looked around, but he couldn't see anything. He felt a frightened little quiver run down his back and up his back.

There was Peter, all by himself on a long walk, and he was as lonely as a dog without a tail.

But Peter was on his way to school at last. So he jumped up and walked bravely. It was a very long walk. After a while he sat down under a tree to rest.

Suddenly he knew someone was watching him. Perhaps it was someone who would play with him.

He turned around and looked around, but he couldn't see anything. He felt a very big scare, just sticking in his throat.

There was Peter all by himself on such a long walk to the village, and he felt as lonely as the sun in the sky.

But Peter was on his way to school at last, and even though he was hot and tired, he went slowly on down the road.

Finally he came out of the tangled trees at the edge of the woods. There was a house and another house. Then there were lots of houses, and Peter knew he had come to the village.

Now he would find someone to play with him!

Peter looked all around at the neat little houses tucked into their flower beds. He saw cars driving along and trucks driving along. He saw people running to get on a bus. He saw a milkman and a mailman. But he didn't see any boys and girls anywhere! Perhaps they were already inside the school.

Then Peter stood still right in the middle of the village. How would he know which building was the

school? He thought he would find it when he saw all the boys and girls playing outside.

Suddenly a lady running for a bus nearly tripped over Peter. "My goodness!" she said. "Are you growing there on the sidewalk?"

"No," said Peter. "I'm looking for the school."

"Well, you're looking right at it," the lady said rather crossly.

Peter didn't tell her he wasn't sure what a school looked like. He crossed the street and walked into the big yard.

There was the school, so white in the morning sunshine it seemed to sparkle. Peter felt as if there were sparkles running around inside him, too.

Here he was at school! Now surely he would find someone to play with him.

But all he saw was an old man sweeping the steps.
Peter ran to him. "Where are all the boys and girls?"

"You're early," the man said.

"No one has come to play yet?" Peter asked.

"No. You must be new. I haven't seen you before."

"No," said Peter proudly. "Today is the first day
I've ever come to school. I was five just yesterday."

"Oh, dear!" said the man, and he sat down on the
steps beside Peter. "You're five and all grown up and
you can't wait to come to school. That's just a shame,
because you look so eager. But I'm afraid they won't
let you come."

"Why?" Peter asked.

"It's a rule," said the man. "Everyone has to start
school in September, all at the same time—like starting a race. You see, now you're five, well, that's really

something! But you'll have to wait until next September and start school the same time as all the other boys and girls who are five. So now you just better run home quick."

Peter was a very brave boy.

Peter didn't cry.

But all his life he'd waited to go to school, and now he had to go home—without anyone to play with him. Very slowly he started on the long walk home.

Peter felt as lonely as a cloud going nowhere.

By the time poor Peter had trudged through the village and back up the long road into the woods, he was so tired he could hardly lift up his feet.

When he came to the big tree where he had rested that morning, he sat down again. He forgot it was the very place where he felt someone was watching him.

Suddenly a little surprise ran down his back and up his back. Someone *was* watching him!

There was a fat little rabbit looking at Peter.

"Hello!" cried Peter. "Would you play with me?"

The rabbit wiggled his ears and twitched his nose and bobbed his head. When Peter started up the road, the rabbit ran along with him for a little way.

"I guess I've found someone to play with after all," said Peter. He felt as happy as a grin.

But suddenly the rabbit jumped into the bushes and out of sight. Poor Peter! He didn't have anyone to play with after all.

When he came to the brook where he had rested that morning, he sat down again. He forgot it was the very place where he felt someone was watching him.

Suddenly a surprise ran up his back and down his back. Someone *was* watching him!

There was a gay raccoon looking at Peter.

"Hello!" cried Peter. "Would you play with me?"

The raccoon looked at him as if he were quite shy, and went back to washing his lunch in the brook. It made Peter hungry to see him eat. So he started up the road again, but the raccoon came and walked along with him a little way.

"I guess I've found someone to play with after all," said Peter. He felt as joyful as a dance.

But suddenly the raccoon swished his tail and jumped into the bushes and out of sight.

Poor Peter! He didn't have anyone to play with after all.

When he came to the rock he had rested on that morning, he sat down again. He forgot it was the very place where he felt someone was watching him.

Suddenly a surprise ran up his back and down his back—and up again. Someone *was* watching him!

There was a little gray fox looking at Peter.

"Hello!" cried Peter. "Would you play with me?"

The fox grinned and waved his tail, and when Peter started up the road, the fox walked along with him a little way.

"I guess I've found someone to play with me after all," said Peter. He felt as gay as a whistle.

But suddenly the fox jumped into the bushes and

out of sight. There was Peter, all alone again on his long walk, and lonelier than he had ever been before.

It was just too much! Peter was so cross and tired he stamped along the road and kicked stones. But before he knew it, there was the gate to his house. And what do you suppose he saw waiting for him?

His cat and his dog and his sheep and his ducks were all at the gate, just waiting for Peter to come home and play with them!

The cat was just waiting for Peter to throw the ball she had in her mouth. The dog was just waiting for Peter to throw the stick he had in his mouth. The sheep were just waiting for Peter so they could play tag with him. The ducks were just waiting for Peter so they could dance with him.

Peter hurried into the yard. He threw sticks for his dog and the ball for his cat. He played tag with the sheep, and he danced with the ducks. Why, he had friends after all, and they all wanted to play with him!

And Peter wasn't sure, but he thought, when he looked quickly behind him, that he saw a rabbit scuttle behind a stone, and a fox rustle into the bushes, and a raccoon run down the path toward the pond.

"Peter!" called his mother. "I've been calling and calling you for breakfast. Where have you been?"

"I went for a long walk," said Peter, "and all by myself I found a lot of friends to play with me."

And do you know, Peter didn't tell his mother that he had gone to school. That's Peter's secret—and yours.

Corally Crothers' Birthday

ROMNEY GAY

Corally Crothers jumped out of bed.
"Today is my birthday," Corally said.
"There must be a present
Waiting for me.
Now I wonder where
Such a package can be."

She put on her slippers,
And then in great haste
She put on the bathrobe
Which tied round her waist.

Then she hunted up high
And she hunted down low,
But there wasn't
A present anywhere,   SO

She looked in the closet
And looked in the hall,
But still she could find
No present at all,   SO

She ran down the stairs
And there on the table
Was a nice big box
With a great big label.

She untied the ribbon,
She took off the paper,
And then how she did
Dance, skip, and caper!
"It's just what I wanted,"
Corally cried.

You can see for yourself
What she found inside.

Doughnuts for Lin

NORA S. UNWIN

Lin was the jolliest Scottie pup.
She had sharp, stand-up ears, big whiskers,
and dark earnest eyes under long eyebrows.

Her tongue was very pink.
Her legs were very short.

And whenever she was specially happy,
her tail wagged in a figure eight.

Lin explored her own garden every morning
when she was let out.
Then she would trot off
and explore the garden next door.

This garden belonged to Mrs. Twinkle.

Mrs. Twinkle was a kind little lady
who loved birds.
In winter she hung up a feeding tray for them.
And every morning
she put out fresh seed or new doughnuts
which she made herself.

The chickadees loved the doughnuts.

Lin loved the chickadees.
She used to like to visit near their feeding tray
and watch them.

But Lin liked doughnuts too.
Sometimes the chickadees dropped pieces
or flipped nearly a whole doughnut
off the tray by mistake.
(When they looked for it on the ground
it would be gone!)

Mrs. Twinkle was sometimes puzzled
to see how fast the doughnuts disappeared.
But then she would go indoors
and make some more.

One day she noticed little four-toed footprints
on the snow under the bird feeder.
She was not pleased.

"I do not like other people to come
into my garden without being invited,"
she said firmly.
"This must be stopped."
So she began to think
of ways and means to keep them out.

Lin wasn't the only visitor.
A big tomcat, who lived three doors away,
began coming to the garden too.

He liked to watch the chickadees also.
He did not care about doughnuts.
He sat much too near the feeding tray
in the shelter of a bush.
He gazed and gazed at the little birds
with his greedy green eyes.
He hoped one would alight on the ground
for a fallen seed. Then he would pounce!

Soon the chickadees felt so uneasy
that they stopped coming to the bird feeder.

This made Mrs. Twinkle very sad.
"Perhaps my doughnuts are not as good
as they used to be," she thought.
"I'll make some more and better ones."

So early next morning
she began mixing and cutting the dough,
ready for more doughnuts.

Then out of the window,
she caught sight of a little black dog
trotting round to her bird feeder.
"Oh, that naughty dog again!
What shall I do?" she wailed.

"Why should I make doughnuts
for a dog to eat? She's plump enough."
Mrs. Twinkle felt quite angry.

But as she watched from her window,
she suddenly saw old Mr. Tomcat
under the bushes.
One single chickadee had come to the feeder.
Seeing no one round,
he had forgotten about the cat,
and dropped to the ground
to peck at a sunflower seed.

Then—pounce!
Mr. Tomcat darted out of his hiding place.
But chickadee was too quick for him.

Just at that moment
Lin came round the corner.

"Aha, Cat!" she barked joyfully,
and gave full chase.

In a moment
Mr. Tomcat was fleeing for his life,
and Lin was on his tail,
barking and squealing with delight.

"That will teach that old cat a lesson,"
thought Mrs. Twinkle. And indeed it did.
Mr. Tomcat never dared
come back to the garden again.

But the chickadees did.
More and more of them came fluttering,
asking for doughnuts.

So Mrs. Twinkle, feeling very happy,
brought out a goodly supply
of her new doughnuts
and put them on the tray.

She even put a specially big one
on the ground for Lin, as a reward
for chasing away the cat.
"Good dog, good dog," she said,
and called Lin to come.

The little dog wagged her tail
and ate the doughnut.

The chickadees twittered.
Everyone felt happy.

From then on, Mrs. Twinkle and Lin
became the greatest of friends.

The Baby House

NORMA SIMON

Once upon a time there were three mothers:
Louise,
Lassie,
and Mother.

There were three fathers too:
Fuzzy,
Lance,
and Daddy.

And then there was me.

All the mothers wanted babies.
All the fathers wanted babies.
And I wanted all the babies.
All of us waited
and waited
and waited.

Louise looked rounder
and rounder
and rounder.

And I helped Daddy make a house for kittens.

The kittens came   1   2   3   4.

That's all.

Louise loved them, licked them, fed them.
All the mothers looked.
All the fathers looked.
And I looked.

All the mothers wanted babies.
All the fathers wanted babies.

And I wanted all the babies.

All of us waited
        and waited
         and waited.

Lassie looked rounder
        and rounder
         and rounder.

And I helped Daddy make a house for puppies.

The puppies came 1 2 3 4 5 6 7.

That's all.

Lassie loved them, licked them, fed them.
All the mothers looked.
All the fathers looked.
And I looked.

All the mothers wanted babies.
All the fathers wanted babies.
And I wanted all the babies.

All of us waited
        and waited
        and waited.

Mother looked rounder
        and rounder
        and rounder.

And I helped Daddy make a new room for baby.

The baby came   1.
That's all.

Mother loved him, kissed him, fed him.
And I helped Mother.

All the mothers looked.
All the fathers looked.
And I looked.

All the mothers had their babies.
All the fathers had their babies.
And I had all their babies.

We loved them, we kissed them, we fed them.

We lived in a baby house.

Bumble Bee

MARGARET WISE BROWN

Black and yellow
Little fur bee
Buzzing away
In the timothy
Drowsy
Browsy
Lump of a bee
Rumbly
Tumbly
Bumbly bee.
Where are you taking
Your golden plunder
Humming along
Like baby thunder?
Over the clover
And over the hay
Then over the apple trees
Zoom away.

Little Lamb

DAHRIS MARTIN

Baba was a lamb.
Baba was a white lamb.
His fleece was soft and warm.
"I am a happy lamb," said Baba.
"My fleece is white as milk,
my fleece is soft as silk,
my fleece is warm as a quilt.
I am a happy lamb
because I have such a beautiful coat."

But one day Baba was sad.
Baba was very, very sad,
for his coat was falling off.
Here a little,
and there a little,
Baba's coat was falling off in pieces.
Just as children lose their baby teeth
Baba was losing his baby fleece.
Here a little,
and there a little,
Baba's coat was falling off,
until parts of Baba were bare.

Parts of him were pink and bare,
and Baba was cold.
"Oh, what shall I do!" he cried.
"I am losing my beautiful coat.
Where can I get another?
I know!
I will go to the merchant.
He will give me a coat."

So Baba went to the merchant and said,
"Merchant, Merchant,
I am losing my coat,
my beautiful coat,
as white as milk,
as soft as silk,
and as warm as a quilt.
Won't you please give me another?"

The merchant looked sorry.
"Alas, little brother," he answered,
"I have no coat to give you.
Go to the tailor.
He will give you a coat."

So Baba went to the tailor and said,
"Tailor, Tailor,
I am losing my coat,
my beautiful coat,
as white as milk,
as soft as silk,
and as warm as a quilt.
Won't you please give me another?"
The tailor shook his head.
"Alas, little brother,
I have no coat to give you.
Go to the weaver.
He will give you a coat."

So Baba went to the weaver and said,
"Weaver, Weaver,
I am losing my coat,
my beautiful coat,
as white as milk,

as soft as silk,
and as warm as a quilt.
Won't you please give me another?"
But the weaver only looked sad.
"Alas, little brother,
I have no coat to give you.
Go to the shepherd.
He will give you a coat."

So Baba went to the shepherd and said,
"Shepherd, Shepherd,
I am losing my coat,
my beautiful coat,
as white as milk,

as soft as silk,
and as warm as a quilt.
Won't you please give me another?"
"Alas, little brother," the shepherd replied,
"I have no coat to give you."

Baba was feeling so bad by this time that
   he began to cry.
"My coat is all ragged.
What shall I do?
I went to the merchant;
he sent me to the tailor.
I went to the tailor;
he sent me to the weaver.
I went to the weaver;
he sent me to you.
And you have no coat for me.
Where shall I go now?
What shall I do?"
The shepherd thought for a while.
Suddenly he smiled.
"I have an idea!
Go to the black sheep, Baba.
He is very wise.
Black Sheep will tell you what to do."

So Baba went to Black Sheep and said,
"Black Sheep, Black Sheep,
I am losing my coat,
my beautiful coat,
as white as milk,
as soft as silk,
and as warm as a quilt.
Won't you please give me another?"
Black Sheep took a good look
at Baba's ragged coat.
Then what do you suppose he did?

He began to laugh.
Black Sheep laughed and laughed,
and laughed and laughed.
Finally he said,
"You do not need a coat, little brother.
Look! You already have a coat."

Baba turned around and looked at himself.
The old fleece was falling off, to be sure.
Here a little,
and there a little.
But in its place
NEW FLEECE WAS GROWING.

Would you believe it!
All Baba's bare spots
were covered with soft little knots
of brand-new fleece.
Baba began to laugh, too.

He jumped and skipped for joy.
And this was the song he sang,
"I have a coat,
a beautiful coat,
a brand-new coat,
as white as milk,
as soft as silk,
and as warm as a quilt!"

When Company Comes

AILEEN FISHER

We fold up the papers
and straighten the chairs,
and whisk extra sweaters
and jackets upstairs,
and help bake the cookies
(and eat all the crumbs),
and polish the silver . . .
   when company comes.

We get out the dishes
we don't often use,
and sweep all the cubbies
and put away shoes,
and dust all the vases
and fiddle-de-dums,
and can't find our playthings . . .
   when company comes.

We use our best glasses,
our candlesticks gleam,
we have little nut-cups,
and cake and ice cream,
and candy and other such
yummy-yum-yums,
but it isn't like OUR house . . .
    when company comes!

Willie's Walk to Grandmama

MARGARET WISE BROWN
AND ROCKBRIDGE CAMPBELL

Willie lived in the City. His Grandmama lived in the
Country. She telephoned him.

"Come to see me," said Grandmama.
"When?" asked Willie.
"Now," said Grandmama.
"How will I get there?" asked Willie.
"Walk," said Grandmama.
"Through the Country?" asked Willie.
"Through the Country," said Grandmama.
"All by myself?" asked Willie.
"All by yourself," said Grandmama.

"I've heard that wild flowers are wild," said Willie.

"They are," said Grandmama, "but come anyway."

"How will I find the way?" asked Willie.

"Follow your nose," said Grandmama.

"How will I know when I get to your house?" asked Willie.

"Look inside and you will see me there," said Grandmama.

And she hung up.

So Willie started out. He walked out of the City and into the Country. He followed his nose. The very first thing he saw was a WILD FLOWER. Should he turn around and go back to the City?

No. Not Willie. He leaned down and sniffed. It smelled like a violet, so he picked it.

And Willie walked on to Grandmama.

The Country looked very big to Willie. There were butterflies in the Country. The butterflies fluttered all around his head. Willie had never seen a butterfly before. Should he turn around and go back to the City?

No. Not Willie. He stood stone still till the butterflies fluttered by. Then he picked a bunch of smelly weeds butterflies wouldn't like.

And Willie walked on to Grandmama.

Then he came to three wild red strawberries. They were almost hidden beneath some very green leaves.

But was Willie afraid of a strawberry?

No. Not Willie. He picked all three strawberries and ate two of them. The other one he put in his pocket.

And Willie walked on to Grandmama.

He came to a shallow stream across the road. There was no bridge. How would he ever get across? Should he turn around and go back to the City?

No. Not Willie. He took off his shoes and socks, and

barefooted he waded right through the cold wet water of the stream. Then he put on his socks and his shoes.

And Willie walked on to Grandmama.

He came to a hill. It was a very high hill. Should he turn around? No. Not Willie. He walked up the hill backwards, so as not to see how high it was.

Then he walked down the hill backwards, so he could see how high the hill had been.

And Willie walked on to Grandmama.

At last he came to a great big house. It had enormous doors. Could this be Grandmama's house?

Willie went and peeked in the enormous doors. The house was full of horses. No Grandmama.

Next he came to a rather small house. It had a little round door in it. Could this be Grandmama's house?

Willie went and peeked in the little round door. The house was full of a big fat dog—sound asleep. No Grandmama.

Then he came to a tiny little house. It had a tiny tiny door. Could this be Grandmama's house? Willie went and tried to peek in, but the door was too small.

He heard a quiet buzzing noise inside, so he knocked to see who lived there. HONEY BEES! No Grandmama.

Then he came to a white house all covered with red roses. It had windows and a green door and a chimney with smoke coming out. Could this be Grandmama's house?

Willie went and peeked in one of the windows.

And there was Grandmama, sitting inside waiting for Willie to come. "Sakes," said Grandmama, "don't stand there. Come on in, child."

And Willie went inside and gave his Grandmama a
great big hug. Then he gave her the wild flower and
the bunch of smelly weeds. "Very pretty," said
Grandmama.

And she gave Willie a glass of milk and a great big
piece of chocolate cake.

"Oh," said Willie, "here is a little wild squashed strawberry for you."

And that was Willie's walk to Grandmama.

Fish

MARY ANN HOBERMAN

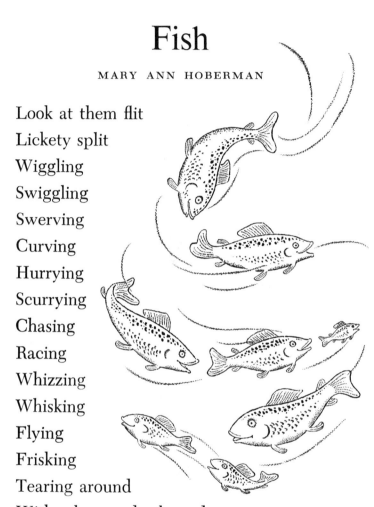

Look at them flit
Lickety split
Wiggling
Swiggling
Swerving
Curving
Hurrying
Scurrying
Chasing
Racing
Whizzing
Whisking
Flying
Frisking
Tearing around
With a leap and a bound
But none of them making the TINIEST
                           TINIEST
                           TINIEST
                           TINIEST
                           SOUND.

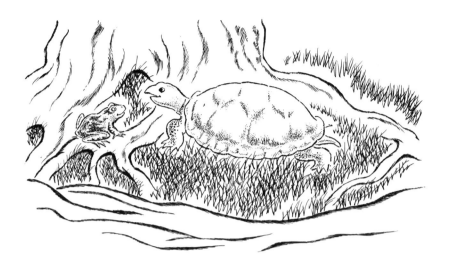

Timothy Turtle

ALICE VAUGHT DAVIS

Timothy Turtle lived in a forest near a river. He was a very old turtle and had lived there for many years. All the animals that lived in the forest knew him and liked him.

But his very best friend was the frog who lived in the roots of a tree on the bank of the stream.

Timothy often took the frog on his back for a ride up the river.

Timothy liked to swim in the water. He liked to sit on the bank and sleep in the sun.

But best of all he liked to slide down a steep bank that was in the forest not far from the river.

One morning Timothy went for a slide. The bank was slippery from a rain that had come in the night. He slid very fast. Just at the bottom of the bank he slipped and rolled over on his back.

Now, Timothy's shell was very heavy, and try as he would, he could not turn over. So he lay on his back kicking his feet in the air. He kicked and kicked and kicked. He tried very hard, but he could not turn his heavy shell over.

The squirrel who lived in the tree nearby saw Timothy. He came to ask what had happened.

"What is the matter, Timothy?" asked the squirrel.

"I fell on my back and can't turn over. Can you help me?" But the squirrel was so little he could not help Timothy.

"I will go and find help," said the squirrel. So he ran into the forest and met the rabbit.

"Come quickly. Timothy Turtle fell on his back and can't turn over."

They ran back to Timothy. But the squirrel and the rabbit could not turn him over.

"I will go and find someone else," said the squirrel. He ran through the forest until he came to the woodchuck's home.

"Come quickly. Timothy Turtle fell on his back and can't turn over."

"I'll be glad to help," said the woodchuck. "Wait till I tell Mrs. Woodchuck where I'm going."

But the squirrel and rabbit and the woodchuck could not turn Timothy over.

"I will go and see if I can find someone else," said the squirrel. He ran into the forest and found the possum sleeping in the sun.

The squirrel shook and shook him until he opened his eyes and looked up.

"Come quickly. Timothy Turtle fell on his back and can't turn over."

"I'll see what I can do," said the possum in a sleepy voice, starting to walk slowly behind the squirrel.

"Will you walk a little faster, Mr. Possum?"

"Certainly," said the possum, walking as fast as he could. So on they went until they came to Timothy.

But the squirrel and the rabbit and the woodchuck and the possum could not turn Timothy over.

They sat looking at the turtle and wondering what to do. Timothy was still kicking his feet in the air and trying to turn over.

Now the frog had heard the noise and came to see what it was about. He sat on the bank nearby and started to laugh. He laughed and croaked so loud that the animals all turned and looked at him.

"What are you laughing about?" asked the squirrel.

"I am laughing at all of you," answered the frog.

"If you think it is so funny, tell us how we can turn Timothy over."

"I will," said the frog. "Just take him by the tail and pull him down to the river. When he falls in the water, he will turn over."

So the possum took hold of Timothy's tail, and the woodchuck took hold of the possum, and the squirrel took hold of the woodchuck, and the rabbit took hold of the squirrel. They pulled and pulled until they got Timothy down to the bank of the river.

Splash! went the water, as Timothy fell in and turned over.

Timothy dived and swam in the water until he had washed the mud from his shell. Then he came out on the bank and thanked his friends for helping him.

The rabbit and the woodchuck and the possum and the squirrel stood on the bank and watched Timothy as he took the frog on his back for a ride up the river.

The Mailman

JAMES L. HYMES, JR.

Mr. Alexander Appleton was a mailman—a very important mailman, too. He was important to the farmers who lived near the town of Hilltop. He delivered their letters, packages, post cards, and magazines.

Mr. Appleton didn't walk from house to house the way city mailmen do. The farmhouses around Hilltop were far apart. Mr. Appleton drove his blue car sixty miles every day to deliver the mail. But he didn't work on Sundays. And he didn't work on holidays either.

Mr. Appleton liked his work.

He liked to drive his car.

He liked the farmers.

But one particular day he was ready to swap jobs

with a cook, a sailor, a shoemaker, or with almost any-one at all. "Trouble-trouble day"—that's what Mr. Appleton called that day.

"Trouble-trouble day" began just like any ordinary day. Mr. Appleton left his house early, just as the sun was rising. He drove his blue car down the highway toward the railroad station. Every morning Mr. Appleton met the early train that brings the mail to Hilltop.

At 6:20 A.M. right on the dot, the mail train rolled to a stop. Right away the mail clerks began to unload the mailbags and packages for Hilltop.

Mr. Appleton watched, and he counted, and he sighed.

"Six bags," he said a little sadly.

Those six bags held a lot of mail—mail which had to be delivered. But six heavy mailbags did not make this a "trouble-trouble day."

Mr. Appleton loaded the mailbags and a box of chicks into his car, and away he went to the post office. He and two other mailmen spent a whole hour sorting the mail. Mr. Appleton arranged all his letters and post cards in just the right order. Then he carried the mail —all sorted now—back to his car.

Sorting the mail wasn't much fun, but sorting the mail didn't make this a "trouble-trouble day." Mr. Appleton was quite cheerful as he climbed into his car.

"Good-by," he called, and he waved gaily to one of the town mailmen.

Mr. Alexander Appleton drove on down the high-way. At Box 1 he stopped and left a letter. Into Box 2 he put an air mail letter and a magazine. Box 3 got two letters and a picture post card.

Mr. Appleton had no mail for Box 4. But he had to stop anyhow because the red flag was up. The red flag was a signal for him to look inside the box.

Mr. Appleton opened Box 4. Inside he found a letter —a letter which the farmer himself had written. The letter was to go to the farmer's son, who was in the army. Mr. Appleton took the letter. It was his job to mail it at the post office in Hilltop.

Mr. Appleton had a package for Box 5—a big pack-age. It was too big for him to squeeze into the mail-box, so he had to drive all the way up the road to the farmer's house. But even the extra drive didn't make this a "trouble-trouble day."

Mr. Appleton blew a loud blast on his whistle. The farmer's boy ran out of the house. On his face was a big wide grin.

"Chicks," said the boy, as he took the box from the mailman.

Mr. Appleton drove on, and then "trouble-trouble day" really began.

At the very next mailbox, which was Box 6, Mr. Appleton stopped. He opened the box to put in some letters. And what do you think flew out right into his face?

"A butterfly!" Mr. Appleton snorted.

He fussed, and he brushed, and he waved it off the tip of his nose.

Mr. Appleton's nose still tickled when he reached Box 7. He stopped his car. The mailbox door was open.

He looked inside, and *more* trouble flew right at him!

"A bird!" moaned Mr. Appleton.

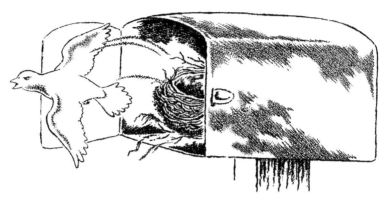

A bird was building her nest right in the mailbox.

How could a man deliver mail if the mailbox became a birdhouse?

Ever so carefully Mr. Appleton opened Box 8, Box 9, and Box 10. By this time he suspected that this day was his "trouble-trouble day."

Then he stopped at Box 11. Slowly, slowly he opened it.

"A bee!" he cried, as a big angry bumblebee flew out of the box and stung him on the hand.

Now you can see why Mr. Appleton was ready to

swap jobs with a cook, a sailor, a shoemaker, or with almost anyone at all.

Box 12 was next. Mr. Appleton had no mail for Box 12. But the red flag was up, so he had to stop.

Very slowly, very carefully, with his hand still hurting from the bee sting, Mr. Appleton opened the box.

"Cake!" he shouted.

Box 12 saved the day.

Mrs. Mary Merrybell, his good friend, had left him a surprise—a big piece of homemade chocolate cake with thick chocolate icing.

One bite of that cake, and Mr. Appleton began to feel much better—all except his hand. It still hurt a little.

Mr. Appleton tooted a thank-you on the horn: "Beep, boop."

He waved to Mrs. Mary Merrybell.

"Good-by!" he called.

And, as he joggled on down the road, he decided that he didn't really want to swap jobs with anyone at all.

6 O'Clock Rooster

MELVERN BARKER

On a little farm in the country lived a family of four: a mother, a father, a little boy, and a cat named Mooch. Every morning very early they all awoke when the rooster crowed.

The father had his work to do.
The mother had her work to do.
The little boy did chores.

They were happy country people.

There was also a family of four who lived in the city.
A father who had his work to do.
A mother who had many things to do.
A little boy who ran errands and a little dog named Pooch who just slept.

112

Every morning very early they all awoke when the street noises began.

They were happy city people.

The country boy and the city boy were cousins. One day the country boy wrote a letter to his city cousin. It said, "Please come and visit me and I will show you how we live in the country."

The city cousin wrote back and said, "I will come; I want to know about the country."

When the city boy arrived they all had a big country supper. Then the two cousins went to bed in a big country bed.

The little country boy fell fast asleep right away. But the little city boy did not, for he heard all kinds of strange noises which kept him awake.

The wind whistled in the trees, the crickets chirped, the gate creaked, the windmill banged, and just as the sun was coming up he heard the loudest noise of all—the rooster crowed. He seemed to say, "Get up, get up, for this is a beautiful day."

Then all was very quiet and the city boy finally got to sleep. He slept until ten o'clock.

When he awoke he thought, "I wish I could be a country boy and get up when everyone else does."

At breakfast the country boy's mother said, "I am glad to see you, but what made you sleep so long?"

"All the noises kept me awake," said the city boy. "And I could not sleep until they stopped early in the morning."

"What noises do you mean?" asked the mother.

The city boy said, "I heard the wind, I heard something chirp, I heard a creaking noise, I heard a bang, and then I heard a very loud funny noise early in the morning. Then all was quiet and I fell asleep."

"Why, those are country noises," said the country boy's mother, "and soon you will be used to them. Now go out and help feed the pigs."

So the city boy joined the country boy and they fed the pigs.

The second night the little city boy went to bed very tired. Again he heard the wind whistle, the gate creak, the cricket chirp, and at daybreak the rooster crowed.

When the rooster stopped crowing he went to sleep and slept until nine o'clock. He got up and had his breakfast. He helped feed the pigs and chickens.

The third night he heard the wind whistle, the gate creak, the crickets chirp, but the noises didn't seem so loud. He went to sleep and slept until the sun came up and the rooster crowed, "Get up, get up." But he didn't get up until eight o'clock. Then he had his breakfast and helped feed the pigs, the chickens, and the calf.

The fourth night he hardly heard the noises at all. When the sun came up and the rooster crowed he only stayed in bed until seven o'clock. He had his breakfast and helped feed the pigs, the chickens, the calf, and the colt.

The fifth night he went to bed and heard no noise at all. He fell asleep and slept the whole night through.

So when the sun came up and the rooster crowed, the little city boy got right up at six o'clock. He had a big country breakfast with all his country cousins.

"The noises have stopped," he said.

Everyone laughed. "The noises haven't stopped," said the country boy's mother, "for last night the wind whistled, the crickets chirped, the gate creaked, and the windmill banged."

"You've just got used to the country noises," said the country boy. "You get up with the six o'clock rooster; so now you're a country boy, too."

Caps for Sale

ESPHYR SLOBODKINA

Once there was a peddler who sold caps. But he was not like an ordinary peddler carrying his wares on his back. He carried them on top of his head.

First he had on his own checked cap, then a bunch of gray caps, then a bunch of brown caps, then a bunch of blue caps, and on the very top a bunch of red caps.

He walked up and down the streets, holding himself very straight so as not to upset his caps.

As he went along he called, "Caps! Caps for sale! Fifty cents a cap!"

One morning he couldn't sell any caps. He walked up the street and he walked down the street calling, "Caps! Caps for sale. Fifty cents a cap!"

But nobody wanted any caps that morning. Nobody wanted even a red cap.

He began to feel very hungry, but he had no money for lunch.

"I think I'll go for a walk in the country," said he. And he walked out of town—slowly, slowly, so as not to upset his caps.

He walked for a long time until he came to a great big tree.

"That's a nice place for a rest," thought he.

And he sat down very slowly, under the tree and leaned back little by little against the tree trunk so as not to disturb the caps on his head.

Then he put up his hand to feel if they were straight —first his own checked cap, then the gray caps, then the brown caps, then the blue caps, then the red caps on the very top.

They were all there.

So he went to sleep.

He slept for a long time.

When he woke up he was refreshed and rested.

But before standing up he felt with his hand to make sure his caps were in the right place.

All he felt was his own checked cap!

He looked to the right of him. No caps.

He looked to the left of him. No caps.

He looked in back of him. No caps.

He looked behind the tree. No caps.

Then he looked up into the tree.

And what do you think he saw?

On every branch sat a monkey. On every monkey was a gray, or a brown, or a blue, or a red cap!

The peddler looked at the monkeys.

The monkeys looked at the peddler.

He didn't know what to do.

Finally he spoke to them.

"You monkeys, you," he said, shaking a finger at them, "you give me back my caps."

But the monkeys only shook their fingers back at him and said, "Tsz, tsz, tsz."

This made the peddler angry, so he shook both hands at them and said, "You monkeys, you! You give me back my caps."

But the monkeys only shook both their hands back at him and said, "Tsz, tsz, tsz."

Now he felt quite angry. He stamped his foot, and he said, "You monkeys, you! You better give me back my caps!"

But the monkeys only stamped their feet back at him and said, "Tsz, tsz, tsz!"

By this time the peddler was really very, very angry. He stamped both his feet and shouted, "You monkeys, you! You must give me back my caps!"

But the monkeys only stamped both their feet back at him and said, "Tsz, tsz, tsz."

At last he became so angry that he pulled off his own cap, threw it on the ground, and began to walk away.

But then, each monkey pulled off his cap . . .

and all the gray caps,

and all the brown caps,

and all the blue caps,
and all the red caps came flying down
out of the tree.

So the peddler picked up his caps and put them
back on his head,

first his own checked cap,
then the gray caps,
then the brown caps,
then the blue caps,
then the red caps on the very top.

And slowly, slowly, he walked back to town calling, "Caps! Caps for sale! Fifty cents a cap!"

Tito's Hats

MELCHOR G. FERRER

There was a boy named Tito. He lived in a house in the mountains of Mexico.

He lived with his father, his grandmother, and his little sister.

Tito had a hat that was old and ragged.

One day while he was on the side of the mountain a wind came and blew his hat away. Tito stood there and watched his hat go off down the side of the mountain.

That night, at supper, his father decided that Tito would go with him to the market on Sunday to buy a new hat.

So Tito went to sleep thinking of new hats and the kind he would like to get.

On Sunday very early in the morning before the sun was up, Tito and his father started for the market.

There were many people on the road to town. They were all going to the market. When the sun came up, Tito and his father could see the town ahead of them.

When they arrived, the market was already filled with people. They tied their burro and went walking through the market.

Whenever they came to a hat store, they went in and Tito tried on the hats.

But they were all either too small or too big.

Then, all at once, just as they left a store, a crowd of men came toward them. When they had passed, Tito could not see his father. All the faces around him were strange, and he could not see his father anywhere.

He went all over the market, looking.

Suddenly he saw an old man who was sitting be-

side a long pole with many hats on it. And there, on the top of the pole, was the very hat Tito had been wanting.

The old man brought it down, but when Tito tried it on, it was just the smallest bit too small.

As he stood holding it and looking at it, his father came walking out of the crowd.

Tito showed him the hat. The old man smiled. But they all saw that the hat was just the smallest bit too small.

Without saying a word Tito's father took him by the hand and led him off through the crowd.

They went across the market place, and up a narrow little street with big cobblestones.

They came up out of the narrow street into a wider one. They went along that until they came to a house with a room which opened on the street.

They went into the room, and there stood a man beside a white chair.

Tito's father put him in the chair and went to sit on the doorstep. The man came near. He had long mustaches, and in his hand he held a pair of shears.

Tito sat still.

The man reached for his head. Then slowly, he brought up the shears . . . and gave Tito the first haircut he had ever had. After it was over Tito got down from the chair. He scratched his head and moved it in a circle.

Then his father gave the man some money and they went off . . . down the wide street, back down the narrow, steep street . . . back into the market . . . and straight to the old man with the hats.

The old man took down the hat and gave it to Tito. It fit him perfectly.

They all laughed when Tito saw that his hair had been cut to make room for the hat. Then his father paid the old man and Tito and his father went and had some lunch.

After they had eaten they looked for presents to take home.

They bought earrings for Tito's grandmother, some colored ribbons and bright beads for his little sister.

Then Tito's father bought him a purple ice from the man with the striped cart.

The bells of the church were ringing when they left the town.

And when they had gone back up the side of the mountain and come home it was dark . . . and supper was ready.

After they had eaten Tito and his father gave the presents, and Tito showed his new hat.

They all admired it, but Tito's little sister held it longest.

Never had she seen such a hat.

It had been a long day, so Tito said good night and thanked his father for his new hat.

Then, as he started for bed, he took his hat with him.

And when he was in bed and ready to go to sleep, he carefully put his new hat over his toes, and as he went to sleep, he could feel it there, through the covers.

The Santa Claus Bears

DOROTHY SHERRILL

Once upon a time there were two teddy bears. Their names were Roly and Poly. They lived with lots of other toys in Santa Claus's big white house 'way up north.

Roly and Poly were very kind little teddy bears and they liked to help Santa Claus in his workshop. And they liked to help Mrs. Santa Claus in her kitchen.

All year long they helped Santa Claus and Mrs. Santa Claus get ready for Christmas. They put reins on the toy horses. They tied bells on the necks of little woolly lambs. They packed the candy canes that Mrs. Santa Claus made.

Finally it was Christmas Eve. Santa Claus got his big red sleigh out of the barn. Roly helped harness the reindeer. Poly polished the sleigh bells until they were as bright as stars. Then all the toys were piled into the sleigh—hundreds and HUNDREDS and H U N - D R E D S of them! Santa cracked his whip and hollered to his reindeer.

Roly and Poly had to hold on tight because they had been so busy tucking in the other toys they hadn't had time to tuck themselves in!

Then, just as they were flying over some big woods, do you know what happened? The wind blew so hard that it blew the two teddy bears right off the sleigh, and they went sailing down DOWN D O W N!

They didn't hurt themselves at all because they landed in a big soft snowbank—ker-fluff! When they crawled out of the snow they looked just like two fat funny snowmen, and they laughed and laughed at each other.

But soon they stopped laughing and said, "Oh dear, now we can't help Santa Claus put toys in the Christmas stockings! We will miss all the fun!" And they began to cry.

At that very minute they heard a tiny squeaky,

squawky noise. They looked up and saw a little bird. He was crying, too! The little bird cried, "Squeak! Squeak! I am sad! This snow has covered all the food in the wood! We birds and animals won't have ANY CHRISTMAS DINNER!"

Roly and Poly said, "Oh, that is AWFUL! Let's hurry and find goodies for everyone. We will play Santa Claus!"

Roly dug in the snow for berries that birds like. Poly found nuts and acorns for the animals. And they both tore their neck ribbons into tiny pieces for the birds to use to trim their nests. They made a sled out of branches and heaped their goodies on it.

Then, with the little bird to show them the way, they started out to play Santa Claus.

They visited every nest and hideaway hole and left presents for everyone. Finally their sled was empty and they were tired and hungry. Then they heard, 'way up in the sky, the ting-a-ling of Santa's sleigh! They jumped up and hollered as loudly as they could. But he was too far away!

But then a nice thing happened. Their little bird friend popped out of his nest and flew up into the sky and told Santa Claus where the kind little teddy bears were.

Of course Santa drove his sleigh right down and picked up the bears and tucked them into the front seat with him. And he gave them each a little piece of candy so they wouldn't be too hungry before they got home.

When they got home Mrs. Santa Claus gave them all turkey and mashed potatoes with gravy, and chocolate ice cream.

And Santa said, "The little bird told me what kind Santa Claus bears you were. I am proud of you! I'm going to give you your own tiny sleigh with two baby reindeer. Then every year you may take Christmas goodies to the little creatures of the woods."

And that is just what happened.

Good Morning

FANNIE R. BUCHANAN

Good morning, sky!
Good morning, sun!
Good morning, little winds that run!
Good morning, trees,
And creeping grass, and brownie bees!
How did you find out it was day?
Who told you night had gone away?
I'm wide awake;
I'm up now, too.
I'll be right out to play with you!

While Susie Sleeps

NINA SCHNEIDER

It is night time. In the house Susie is asleep. Next to the bed her dolls are tucked in their cribs and her puppy is curled up on the rug. He is sleeping, while Susie sleeps.

Downstairs in the living room, Susie's Daddy and Mommy are awake. Some friends are visiting them. They are talking about grown-up things.

Soon they will be sleepy too. The friends will go home, and Mommy and Daddy will go upstairs and peep into Susie's room. Then they will go to bed and sleep, while Susie sleeps.

Under the eaves the gray and blue pigeons are still. All day long they coo and peck and flutter, but now they are tired. Their heads are tucked under their wings and they are cuddled together sleeping, while Susie sleeps.

The moon is shining brightly into the window. Susie opens her eyes for a moment. The moon is too high for a long-necked giraffe to reach. Two birds couldn't catch it. An airplane can't fly so high. Susie closes her eyes. Everyone in the house is asleep.

But down in the kitchen there is a scratching, scratching noise. It is a furry gray mouse come out of his hole to nibble the crumbs left in the corner. He eats, while Susie sleeps.

Out in the garden the butterflies have folded their wings and the flowers have folded their petals. The busy buzzing bees aren't buzzing any more. They are all asleep in the garden.

But the fireflies fly, and the glowworms glow and the soft-flying moths are wide awake in the moonlight. The bullfrogs in the pond are croaking, grumph, grumph, grumph. Little animals crawl and scurry and hurry about their little animal business in the night. They are awake and busy, while Susie sleeps.

Down in the town, the street lights shine softly. A cat comes silently on its soft cat feet. On the corner is a policeman, watching the stores and houses and the street. He takes good care of things while people sleep.

Floating down the wind, there is a sweet warm smell. The cat smells it. The policeman sniffs it. What can it be?

It is the smell of bread, baking in the bakery.

Men in white aprons and tall funny hats are patting and rolling dough and banging oven doors. Out of the ovens come brown loaves of bread and crisp round rolls for people who will be hungry in the morning. The bakers work, while Susie sleeps.

A little truck backs up to the bakery door to take fresh bread to grocery stores. All through the night trucks roll along with fruit and vegetables and eggs and country food for the city. Big trucks rumble over the roads with their bright headlights shining a path through the dark, while Susie sleeps.

Deep in the dark in the middle of the night long trains speed past houses full of sleeping people. Some trains are going to far places, so far that the people riding in them go to bed and sleep while they rush through the night. But the engineers are not asleep. Oh no! Wide awake engineers drive the trains, while Susie sleeps.

And milkmen are awake all night. Milkmen are churning butter, filling bottles with fresh white milk, and little bottles with cream. And milkmen, driving through the night with milk and cream for breakfast, drive their trucks and wagons, while Susie sleeps.

In a building near the river slam-banging machines are slam-banging as printers print the morning paper that a boy will leave at Susie's house, while Susie sleeps.

Now the world is getting lighter as morning comes. The stars and moon are fading in the sky. The bugs and birds and beasts that are awake all night are going to their holes and nests and homes. They are cuddling into their sleeping places, while Susie sleeps.

Soon the sun begins to warm the garden. The bees are stirring, the flowers are opening, and the butter-flies are awaking, while Susie sleeps.

The pigeons are cooing. One flies to Susie's window sill. The puppy stretches and scratches his ear because he feels morning coming. Susie opens one eye and sees the pigeon's pink feet. She opens the other eye and sees shining dots of sunlight dancing on her wall. Is Susie sleeping?

The puppy pulls at Susie's blanket to wake her up. All around clocks are ringing and voices are talking and feet are walking. The men who worked at night are going home. Mommy and Daddy are getting up. Susie lies in bed and hears a door open. What is that? It's mother taking in the milk from the doorstep and the newspaper from the mat, while Susie is waking.

There's a beat, beat, stir, stir noise in the kitchen. Is that the mouse? And sniff, sniff, there's a bacon toast smell coming up the stairs. And you know that is break-fast. And there's a door opening and a puppy patter-ing and a little girl saying, "Good morning, everybody." And you know—that's Susie, wide awake.

About the Child Study Association of America

The Child Study Association of America is a nonprofit organization which has, since 1888, been carrying on a program to help parents bring up their children with wisdom and enjoyment through the full use of the best knowledge available. Its program of professional training and consultation for those who work with families, its publications, lectures, parent discussion groups, and counseling services offer guidance for wholesome family life.

The Children's Book Committee of the association issues an annual list of its selections after carefully reviewing all the books currently published. Out of the committee's long years of experience have come several story collections welcomed by parents and children alike: *Read-to-Me Storybook, Read Me Another Story, Read Me More Stories, Holiday Storybook, Read to Yourself Storybook, More Read to Yourself Stories, Castles and Dragons,* and *Read to Me Again.*